foods
from around the world
A coloring book
By: Christine Rai

weekend squad
Presents: :D

With every book purchased, we will support a classroom in an underserved community

Bad Words from Around the World by Christine Rai

Published in 2016 by Weekend Squad Inc.

Copyright © 2016 by Christine Rai. All rights reserved.

weekendsquad.com

ISBN: 978-0-9981047-0-6

10 9 8 7 6 5 4 3 2 1

I do not mean to suggest that simply overhearing a foreign tongue adds to one's understanding of that language.

I do know, however, that being exposed to the existence of other languages increases the perception that the world is populated by people who not only speak differently from oneself but whose cultures and philosophies are other than one's own.

Perhaps travel cannot prevent bigotry but by demonstrating that all people cry, laugh, eat, worry and die, it can introduce the idea that if we try to understand each other, we may even become friends.

—Maya Angelou

OH SHIT.

HEY!

Thanks for getting this, it's super cool you like something I made and now we can collaborate to make something new with this coloring book.

So, here's a collection of 38 swear words I drew from a bunch of languages and cultures, including my own. I first got interested in swear words from around the world (aside from them being fun) because unlike other parts of language and customs; profanity, expletives, and insults are a universally human thing we all use.

Some of the expletives in this book have complex meanings with nuances I didn't fully explain in the definitions; instead I included the parallel sentiment we'd use here in New York. And I included some geographical locations other than the United States where you can hear people sayin' these words, in case you're curious about language geography (I am). I'm all about equal opportunity insults so I curated this to only include words that can be used on anyone; nothing racist, homophobic, or misogynistic.

I hope this book puts a smile on your face, teaches you something, inspires you, or helps you express some of your creativity.

At the end of the day, this is a book full of bad words, so live your life, do what you want, color outside the lines if that's what you're into—or, don't color anything at all. Leave it on a table and impress your house guests with your understated coolness.

YOU'RE THE BEST!
enjoy

Christine

~high five~

अरे बकचोनर
arey bakchonar

[AH-rehy BAK-choh-nahr]

phrase

definition: you dumbfuck
language: Bhojpuri
geography: India, Pakistan, Nepal, Guyana, Fiji, Mauritius, Suriname, South Africa, Caribbean

1

바보
babo

[PAH-boh]

noun

definition: stupid, idiot, fool, or blockhead; can be used as a light hearted or severe insult

language: Korean

geography: Korea

3

backpfeifengesicht

[bach-feef-en--gisch]

noun

definition: a face badly in need of a fist

language: German

geography: Germany

5

ばか
baka

[BAH-ka]

noun, adjective

definition: fool, idiot, or stupid

language: Japanese

geography: Japan

برا نيك

bara nayik

[ba-rah nai-ehk]

phrase

definition: fuck off

language: North African dialect of Arabic

geography: Tunisia, Algeria, Libya

9

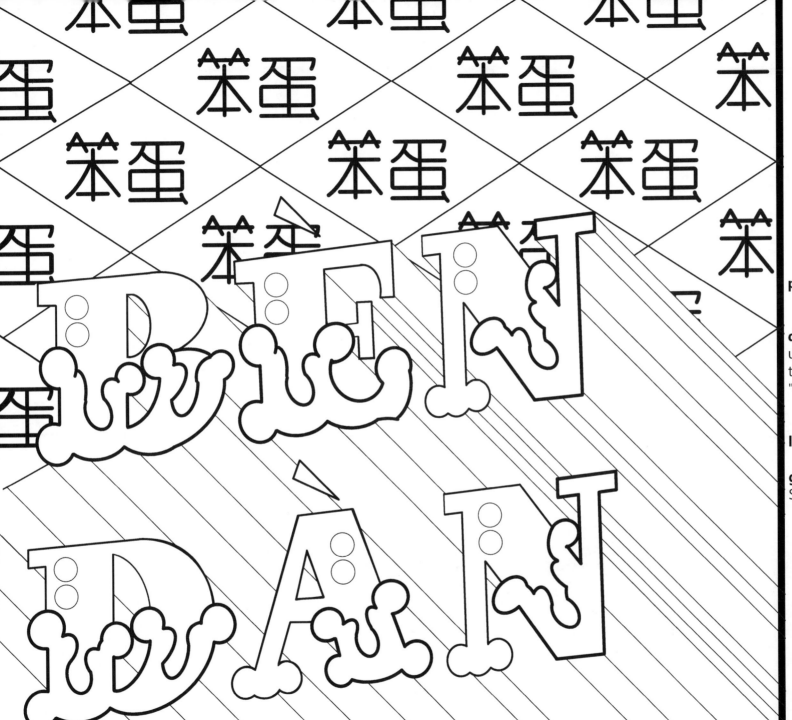

笨蛋
bèn dàn

[ben dahn]

phrase

definition: "stupid egg", it is usually used lightheartedly with the same applications as "dummy", "fool", or "idiot"

language: Mandarin

geography: China, Taiwan, Singapore

11

bitch

[cross your thumb over the palm of your dominant hand to make the letter B, with the index finger against chin, bring hand down]

noun

definition: abrasive, unpleasant person; bitch

language: American Sign Language

geography: deaf communities from the United States of America

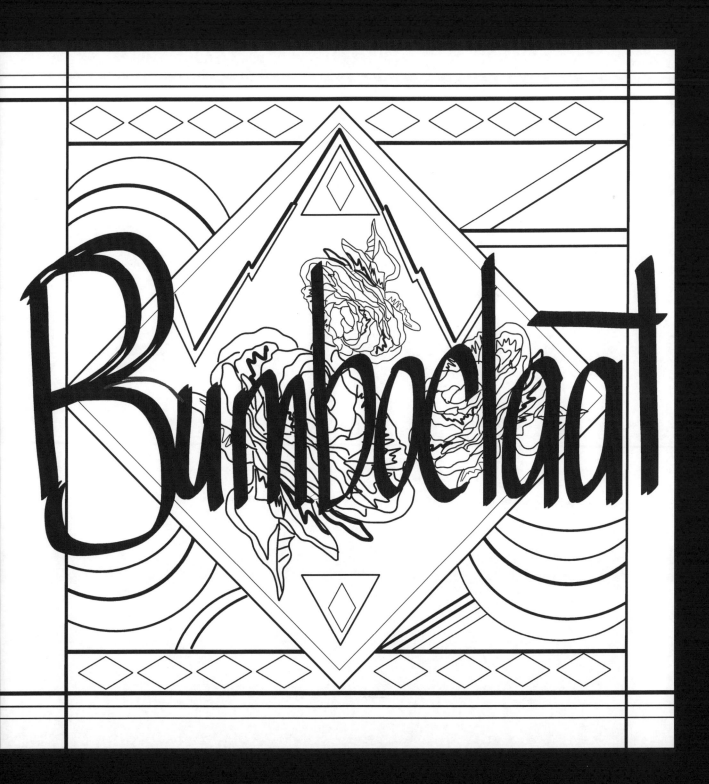

bumboclaat

[bum-boh-CLAAT]

noun, expletive

definition: "Bottom cloth", referring to a cloth used to wipe genitals. It is a versatile word usually used as an exasperation and term of contempt, can be used lightheartedly or seriously and has the same application as "fuck" or "fucker".

language: English

geography: Jamaica, Caribbean communities in the US, UK, Canada

15

cabrão

[cah-BROW]

noun

definition: literally translates to cuckold but it is usually used as a term of contempt or an exasperation and has the same application as "motherfucker" or "bastard"

language: Portuguese

geography: Portugal, Brazil

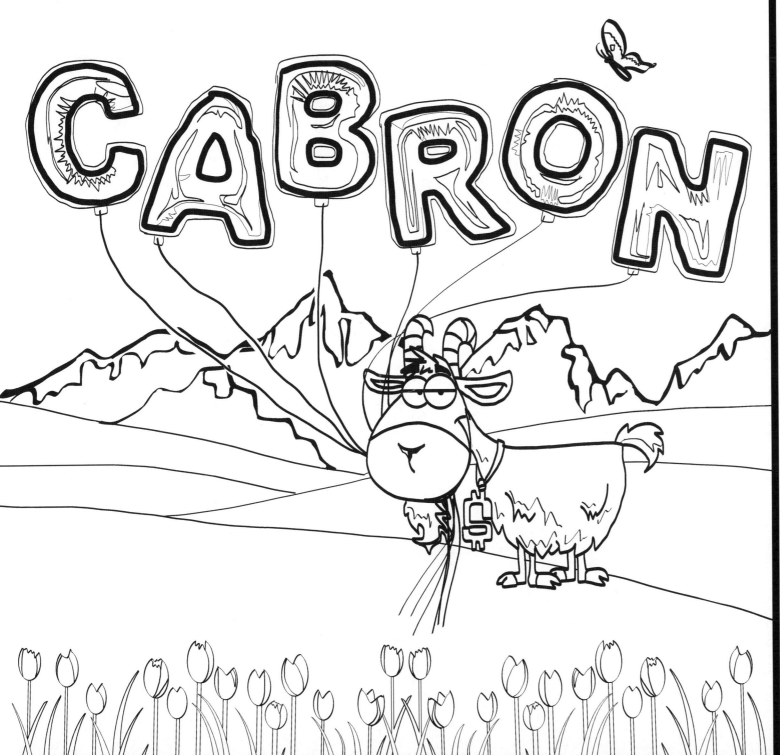

cabrón

[cah-BROW]

noun

definition: literally translates to male goat but has the same application as "cuckold", "asshole", "dick", "bastard", "bitch", or "dude" depending on context, familiarity, geography, and delivery

language: Spanish

geography: Mexico, Spain, Guatemala, Honduras, El Salvador, Nicaragua, Costa Rica, Panamá, Colombia, Venezuela, Ecuador, Perú, Bolivia, Chile, Paraguay, Uruguay, Argentina, Cuba, Puerto Rico, Dominican Republic

19

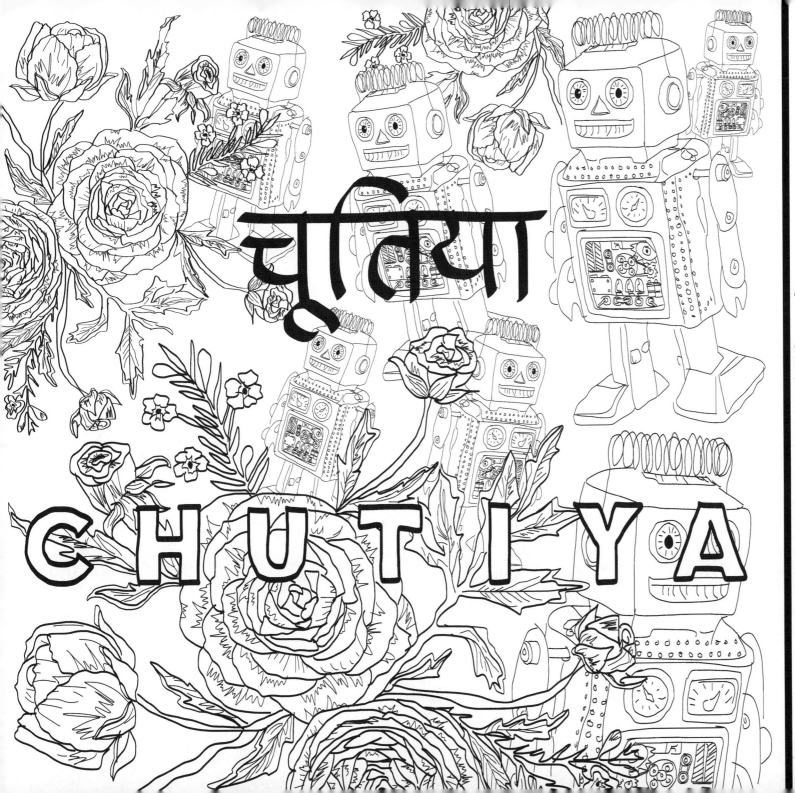

चूतिया
chutiya

[CHOOT-ya]

adjective

definition: slang term that literally translates to "out of the vagina" but has the same applications as "idiot", "fool", "douchebag"

language: Urdu

geography: India, Pakistan

21

demerde toi

[deh-mehrd tuh]

phrase

definition: literally translates to "de-shit yourself", it's a vulgar synonym of "figure it out for yourself"

language: French

geography: France, Belgium, Canada, Haiti, Cameroon, Chad, Luxembourg, Burundi, Switzerland

23

ewure oshi

[you-REH OH-shee]

noun

definition: literally translates to "stupid goat", it can be used as a term of contempt and has the same applications as "jerk" or "idiot"

language: Yoruba

geography: countries of West Africa including Nigeria, Benin, Togo, Senegal, Ghana, Cote d'Ivoire, and the Gambia

25

fakakta

[fah-KAHK-tuh]

adjective

definition: shitty; fucked up

language: Yiddish

geography: Central Europe, Ukraine, Israel, United States

feck

[fah-KAHK-tuh]

adjective

definition: milder synonym to "fuck", it is in the spectrum of "flip" and "fuck", but not as vulgar as "fuck"

language: English

geography: England, Scotland, Wales, Ireland

29

干你的
gan ni de

[gahn nee deh]

phrase

definition: fuck you

language: Mandarin

geography: China, Taiwan, Singapore

haltu kjafti

[HAL-too KAUF-tee]

phrase

definition: literally translates to "hold your mouth" or "keep your mouth shut" and can have the same application as "shut the fuck up"

language: Icelandic

geography: Iceland

33

ha mut

[ha muht]

phrase

definition: "eat shit" but can have the same applications as "shut up" depending on delivery

language: Albanian

geography: Albania, Kosovo, Montenegro, Macedonia, Greece

hitto

[HEH-toe]

expletive

definition: damn

language: Finnish

geography: Finland

37

je m'en fous

[jeh moh foo]

phrase

definition: I don't give a fuck; I don't care

language: French

geography: France, Haiti, Belgium, Canada, Cameroon, Chad, Luxembourg, Burundi, Switzerland

39

klere

[klehr]

expletive, adjective, adverb

definition: Popular Dutch profanity are based around names of diseases, this slang term translates to cholera and has the same applications as "damn" or "fuck".

language: Dutch

geography: Netherlands, Belgium, Suriname

41

לך תז דיין
lekh tizdayen

[leackh tihz-di-en]

phrase

definition: go fuck yourself, fuck you

language: Hebrew

geography: Israel

malakas

[mah-LA-kah]

noun, adjective

definition: "wanker", a person who masturbates (to wank); it is commonly used to mean idiot, jerk, douche, dick, bro, or dude depending on context and delivery

language: Greek

geography: Greece, Cyprus, Albania, Lebanon, Syria, Armenia, Romania, Ukraine

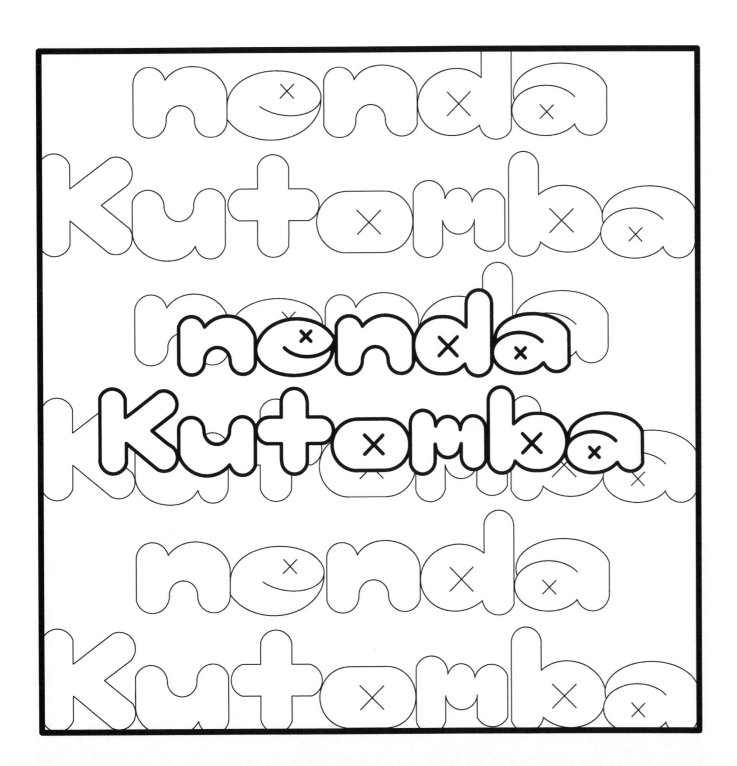

nenda kutomba

[NEN-dah ku-TOM-bah]

phrase

definition: go fuck yourself

language: Swahili

geography: Eastern African countries including Kenya, Tanzania, Uganda, Democratic Republic of Congo, Zambia, Mozambique, Malawi, Rwanda and Burundi, Somalia

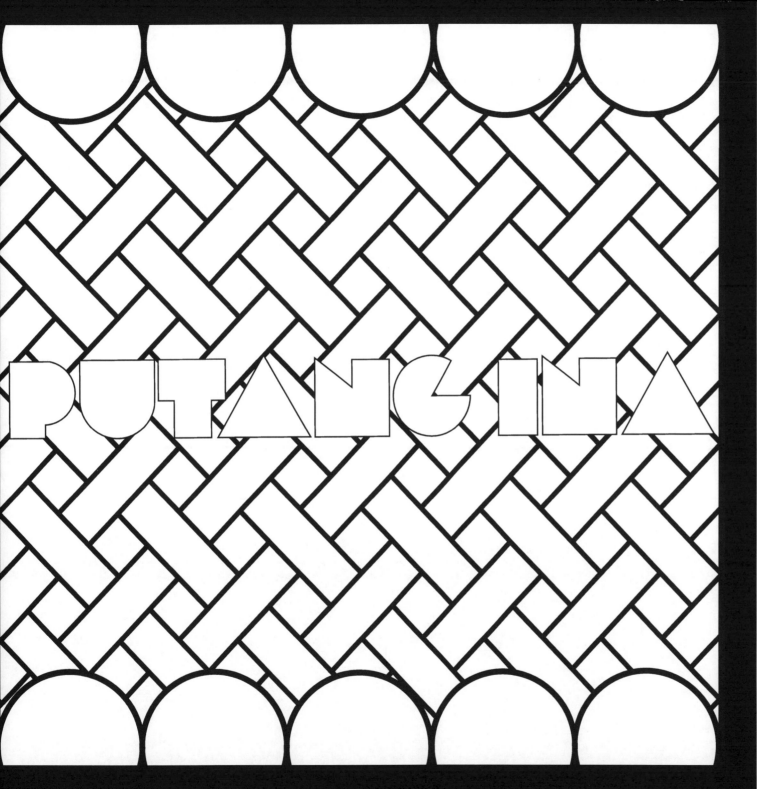

putangina

[POOH-tahng-ee-nah]

noun, expletive

definition: roughly translates to bitch mother, has the same applications as "motherfucker" or "son of a bitch" and can be used as an exasperation with the same applications as "fuck"

language: Tagalog

geography: Philippines

rass

[rahwss]

noun

definition: comes from the phrase "you rass" which literally means "your ass", usually used in a light hearted manner or as a term of endearment

language: English

geography: Guyana, Trinidad, Jamaica, Caribbean, West Indies

root

[root]

verb, noun

definition: fuck

language: English

geography: Australia, New Zealand

silbabot

[sil-BAH-bawt]

adjective

definition: literally translates to "you are the fatty layer on my warm milk" but it has the same application as calling someone a nuisance

language: Amharic

geography: Ethiopia

skunt

[skuhnt]

noun

definition: Comes from the British phrase "mother's cunt". It is a versatile word that can be used lightheartedly or seriously and has the same applications as "motherfucker".

language: English

geography: West Indies, Guyana, Trinidad, Caribbean

57

spierdalaj

[speer-DAH-lai]

phrase

definition: fuck off

language: Polish

geography: Poland

59

stultus

[STOOL-toos]

adjective

definition: slow-witted; stupid

language: Latin

geography: Roman Empire

STULTUS

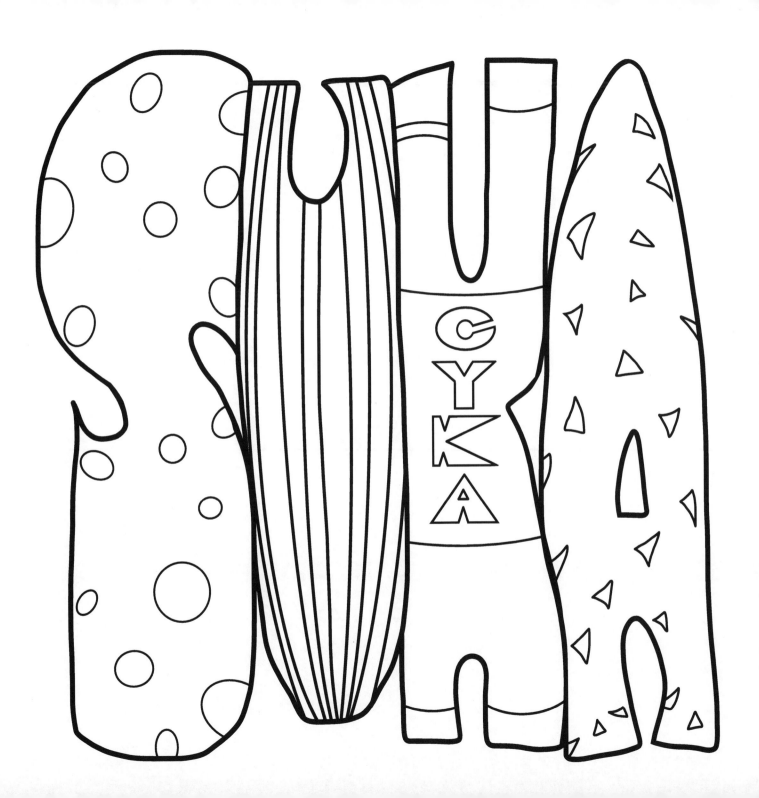

с у к а
suka

[SOO-kah]

noun

definition: literal translation is female dog or bitch and has the same applications as "bitch"

language: Russian

geography: Russia, Ukraine, Poland, Tajikistan, Estonia, Armenia, Azerbaijan, Lithuania, Moldova, Uzbekistan, Kazakhstan, Belarus

tabarnak

[tah-bahr-NAHCK]

expletive

definition: Literally translates to "tabernacle", but words related to the Catholic church are used as profanities in Quebec. This can have the same application as "fuck", "damn", or "shit".

language: French Canadian

geography: Quebec

tosikko

[toh-sic-oh]

adjective

definition: a humorless person who can't take a joke, synonymous to "buzzkill", "uptight"

language: Finnish

geography: Finland

trilkop

[TRIL-kawp]

noun

definition: dickhead

language: Afrikaans

geography: South Africa

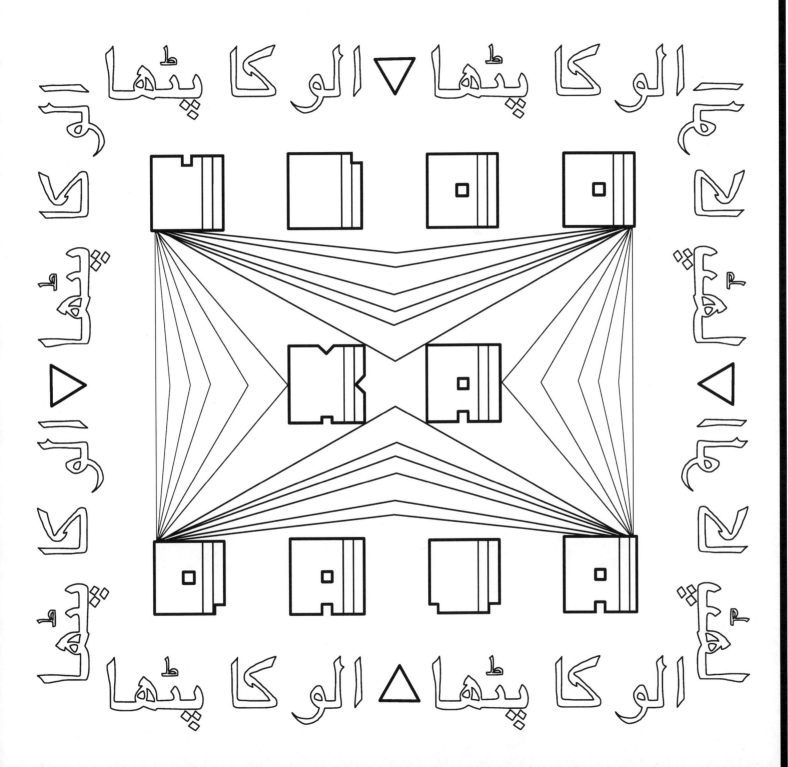

الو کا پٹھا
uloo ka pata

[ooh-loo kah pah-ta]

noun

definition: Literally translates to "son of an owl" but has the same application as "scumbag", "asshole", or "jerk".

language: Hindi, Urdu

geography: India, Pakistan

vaffanculo

[vah-faun-KU-loh]

verb

definition: literally means "go do it in the ass", has the same applications as "fuck off" and "fuck you"

language: Italian

geography: Italy

73

wanker

[WANG-ker]

noun, adjective

definition: The term refers to a person who masturbates (to wank) but is commonly used to mean "idiot", "jerk", "douche", "dick", "bro", or "dude" depending on context and delivery.

language: English

geography: England, Scotland, Wales, Ireland, Australia, New Zealand

test page

test page

test page

merci beaucoup

বহুত ধন্যবাদ্

muchas gracias

ありがとう

grazie mille

감사합니다

mahalo nui loa

THANK YOU!

I hope you liked the book! Show me your colored in work on instagram!
(if you want, no pressure though)

[Instagram icon] @mycursesincursive

and check out what I'm up to at
weekendsquad.com

Made in the USA
Middletown, DE
14 December 2016